No part of this book may be reproduced by any mechanical, photographic or electronic process, or in the form of a phonographic recording; nor may it be stored in a retrieval system, transmitted or otherwise be copied for public or private use, other than for 'fair use' as brief quotations embodied in articles and reviews, without prior written permission of the publisher.

The author of this book does not dispense medical advice or prescribe the use of any technique as a form of treatment for physical or medical problems without the advice of a physician, either directly or indirectly. The intent of the author is only to offer information of a general nature to help you in your quest for emotional and spiritual wellbeing. In the event that you use any of the information in this book for yourself, which is your constitutional right, the author and the publisher assume no responsibility for your actions.

YOUR BODY, ONLY BETTER
Discover, quickly and easily, how and
why your mind can control pain
and speed up healing.
By Mark Baker

Published by Mark Baker.

Copyright © 2015 Mark Baker
All rights reserved.

ISBN: 978-0-9933275-0-6

Thank you

I would like to express my appreciation to everyone who has contributed to my journey up to the point of writing this book, with you this book has become possible.

And to you, the reader, thank you for purchasing and reading this book. To show my appreciation, you can receive free bonus material by visiting *www.possiblemind.co.uk/book-bonus/*

Acknowledgement

A big thank you to Lisa Batty and her red pen for checking and correcting spelling and grammar errors on my part - there were quite a few! I hope you will look back at this book as the first of many that you have proofread, I think it is your calling in life.

Contents

Foreword by Tim Cridland　　4

Introduction　　7

Chapter 1 - 50 Reasons why you can control pain with your mind.　　11

Chapter 2 - 50 Techniques to help you control pain with your mind.　　62

Chapter 3 - 50 Examples of people healing their body with their mind.　　113

Chapter 4 - 50 Techniques to help the body recover using the mind.　　164

Sources　　215

Foreword by Tim Cridland

Pain control has been my profession for over 20 years and I am grateful to be asked to write this foreword. I present pain control as an unusual style of entertainment - in the context of my show, my act is an entertaining and shocking exhibition that gives the same kind of thrill that attracts people to rollercoasters and scary movies. People who come to my show want to be entertained first and foremost, but there is a serious side to what I do. The book you now possess is for people who have an interest this aspect - the methodology of pain control - and it will guide you to some incredible information on using your own mind to control pain and improve health.

Over the years, I have been tested by Dr. Joshua Prager from the UCLA Pain Medicine Center. In one test, filmed for a Japanese TV network, I was put in an fMRI machine that scanned my brain while I was put in pain. The tests showed that although the part of my brain that feels pain was functioning normally, the part of the my brain that is associated with the suffering aspect of pain was dormant.

Dr. Prager would later say "... what Tim can do is he can accurately turn off the suffering by getting himself into a certain state. So that, even though we see that pain information is getting right to the place where you feel it, the whole experience of the suffering, hurting, gets turned off. So he doesn't hurt, so he can take as much pain as he wants."

What Dr. Prager is calling "suffering" is what I was calling "reacting". I have told people that I feel pain the same as anyone else, but that I can chose to react to it differently and that my internal reaction to pain actually changes the whole pain experience. The test with the fMRI showed what I had known intuitively for years.

For the most part, we have very little control of the outside world but everyone can control the way they react internally, and the way you react to the world can change the way the world reacts to you.

In the pages of this book are resources that can help you learn to control your internal state - the goal is to control pain, but that is just one of the uses of these techniques.

The world is bombarding us with stimuli constantly, painful and otherwise. If there is one thing to be learned it is that you have more control over yourself than you are aware of. It has been pointed out that the techniques of internal management that can be used for pain-control are a loophole in Behaviorism - the science that says we are nothing more than a product of external reward/punishment conditioning and internal genetics. Although these are strong factors in human behavior, the fact that we learn to reduce and override something seemingly as controlling as pain shows that we are more than machines made of flesh and blood; that we can actively control who we are.

Mark Baker is one of the few people I have met who is actively pursuing the many methods of mental pain control and self-healing. He is an engaging, sincere person and I have learned some things from him, as I am sure you will, reading this book.

Tim Cridland
As seen on Channel 4 & The Discovery Channel
www.astoundingshow.com

Introduction

Over many years I have developed an interest in the potential of the mind, reading many books, blogs and websites, as well as attending training courses and watching and learning all I can on the subject.

The information I found from these various sources are very interesting but spread wide and far. With this in mind, the type of book I would have liked at the beginning of my journey would have been an overview of the subject, sharing research, examples and techniques. This would have helped develop my understanding and belief in the mind's ability to assist with pain and recovery much sooner.

This book aims to be that book - a great way to introduce you to the subject of the mind and how it can help you gain control of pain and healing. By reading this book, I hope you develop a belief in the power of the mind and its ability to affect the body. By collating all the information into bite-size chunks, with 'learn more' links to other, more in-depth, books, this book has the potential to help you extend and grow your knowledge on this subject very quickly.

When I see all the evidence, and the many ways that the mind has helped others with pain and healing, I cannot help but be inspired and wonder why it is not being utilised further, but that is for another day, or perhaps another book.

My journey into this subject started in the early 2000s, at a point when I was very low and considering suicide. I was in therapy for what turned out to be over 2 years. I would not blame anyone for me being in that situation as it was me that had made my choices, however young, leading up to that point. My therapist, Clive suggested, that with my mindset, I read a book called 'You Can Heal Your Life' by Louise L Hay. This, along with a conversation with a deputy manager at work, was the turning point of my life. I had started to learn to take control of my life, instead of reacting to it. The reason I share this part of my story is that pain and illness can feel a lot like it controls our lives, when in fact we have a lot more control over our emotions, events and outcomes than we first think. For example, we can choose to forgive, to change a perspective, a new daily routine, or a change to our diet, to name a few. We really do have more power than we think, but I believe you are on that journey already because you are reading this right now.

From Louise Hay's book, the journey took me to a knowledge-gaining stage learning all I could from all the sources I could find, including Dr David Hamilton, Jon Kabat Zinn, Shinzen Young, Joseph Murphy, Ernest Rossi, Norman Cousins, Dr Angel Escudero, Hratch Ogali and now, most importantly, the Buddha, who has much to say on the topic of overcoming pain and suffering.

My particular journey then directed me to qualify as a Hypnotherapist, choosing to specialise in Pain Management, Recovery and Performance, before completing several courses including Mindfulness, Basic Buddhism, and a very interesting course in a pain management technique called Noesitherapy.

I am now volunteering for The Samaritans, which has taught me so much about life, as well as running my website on the subject of mind power to help with Pain Management, Recovery and Performance. The website led me to write this book, which I hope you like and find as helpful for your own journey.

Metta,
Mark
www.possiblemind.co.uk

Chapter one

50 Reasons why you can control pain with your mind.

No More Morphine

During WW2, Henry Beecher ran out of Morphine whilst treating US soldiers injured in battle. He continued injecting with just saline: 40% of the soldiers reported pain relief from the placebo.[1]
learn more: http://amzn.to/10yu2j3

Operation No Pain

During the latter part of the last century, Master Hypnotist and Surgeon Jack Gibson carried out many operations using hypnosis as the only painkiller.[2]

"People today can still have operations with hypnosis as their only painkiller."

Reason two

Cancer Pain

Milton Erickson once helped a Cancer patient in excruciating pain to eliminate the sensation, by getting her to hallucinate a lion coming towards her.[3]

three

Hypno Pain Control

A 2001 study proved that hypnosis can increase and decrease chronic pain by changing our perspective and experience of the pain.[4]

Expectancy of Pain

A study using a Magnetic Resonance Imaging (MRI) scanner showed that 40% of the pain comes from the expectancy of that pain.[5]

Metaphors for Pain

A 2013 study showed that using metaphors to explain a person's pain is a much more effective way to help the patient understand and deal with their pain.[6]

"Here is an example I like - chronic pain is like when a doorbell is pressed once but gets stuck and rings constantly."

Meditation and Pain

A North Carolina study showed that one hour's meditation training helped participants reduce pain by almost 50%. The pain relieving effects were considered even greater than those of morphine![7]

"Most people can learn to meditate and gain even more control over their pain."

Migraine Pain

In its first 6 months, a 1975 migraine trial showed that medication and hypnosis were equally as good as each other at controlling pain. In the second 6 months of the trial hypnosis was much better, and in the final 3 months many more patients had cured their migraine than those taking medication.[8]
learn more: http://amzn.to/1pRDPpi

Methods

Hilgards & Hilgards, in their 1983 study, concluded that the 3 most popular ways to control pain are: direct suggestion of pain reduction; changing the experience of pain; moving the attention away from the pain.[9]
learn more: http://amzn.to/1pRDPpi

Reframe Pain

Therapist Mark Tyrrell helped a client reframe his pain from a 'burning sensation' to 'lukewarm' then to a much more manageable 'cool sensation'.[10]

Reason ten

Pain Placebo

The University of California was first to prove that when a painkilling placebo was taken, the brain produced its own natural analgesics, which were like the body's own version of Morphine.[11]
learn more: http://amzn.to/1rV5Ama

eleven

Heat Pain

Research shows that over 70% of people had reduced their sensitivity to heat after taking a placebo. Scans of the brain proved there was less brain activity in the area that reacts to pain.[12]

learn more: http://amzn.to/1rV5Ama

Reason twelve

Statement of Intent

A Fabrizio Benedetti study found that when a placebo was given without an explanation the pain was not reduced. When the placebo was issued with the statement "I am going to give you a painkiller, your pain will subdue after some minutes..." the pain reduced.[13]

learn more: http://amzn.to/1rV5Ama

Dental Injection

Two groups both received a placebo tablet to control the pain of a forthcoming injection. The 1st group were told that the tablet may or may not work. The 2nd group were told how amazing the tablet was at controlling the pain of the injection. The 2nd group experienced less pain and anxiety.[14]
learn more: http://amzn.to/1rV5Ama

Reason fourteen

Finger Pain

A 1996 University of Connecticut study compared application of a placebo cream to ease pain. Volunteers believed the cream to be an analgesic and it was applied to one index finger - when pain was introduced to both index fingers, the finger with the cream applied was shown to be more resistant to pain.[15]
learn more: http://amzn.to/1rV5Ama

Civilian Pain vs War Time

Henry Beecher, a doctor in WW2, found that, compared to civilians, soldiers had a higher threshold to pain and needed less Morphine for the same types of injuries. He concluded that this was due to how their circumstances would change due to the injury - the soldier will be out of harm's way, whereas in civilian life the person may stress over getting to work, providing for their family and medical expenses.[16]

learn more: http://amzn.to/Z1gs6j

"This suggests to me that if we can control our emotional response to our pain, we are then able to focus on controlling our pain as a pure physical sensation."

Reason sixteen

Childbirth Relaxation

As far back as the 1930s, Dr Dick-Read concluded that during childbirth fearful mothers were more tense and felt more pain because blood was being diverted to the vital organs instead of the uterus.[17]
learn more: http://amzn.to/1rVMzkR

seventeen

Operation Relaxation

Published in the Western Journal of Medicine, a study of recovery from pain compared two groups of awake but sedated patients. One group received attention and general care, while the other group had the same care but with guided meditation - the final group recovered quickest, with less pain, anxiety and medication.[18]
learn more: http://amzn.to/1rVMzkR

Reason eighteen

Trees and Water

Dr Roger Ulrich discovered that heart surgery patients in intensive care could be more relaxed and need less pain medication if they looked at pictures of nature with trees and water. This is in comparison to a control group who were shown random abstract pictures.[19]
learn more: http://amzn.to/1rVMzkR

nineteen

Move Your Pain Away

University College London research found that movement and pain are processed in the same part of the brain: a lot of movement desensitises the experience and feeling of pain.[20]

"This could be why we hop around when we stub our toe, or frantically wave our hand if we burn it - this study indicates these actions reduce our pain."

Reason twenty

Strike a Pose

University College London found that adopting a random and unusual arm or leg position will reduce the pain you are feeling. It concluded that odd positioning of the legs and arms inhibited the brain from transmitting the pain.[21]

"Have you noticed that when people are in pain they sometimes return to the fetal position? It looks like this unusual position may help with the pain."

twenty one

Phantom Pain

Les Femi PhD discussed how a patient of his could still feel pain in a leg which had been amputated due to a traffic accident. He stated that around 95% of all amputees still feel pain in the missing limb.[22]
learn more: http://amzn.to/1CKbfiC

"This shows that the brain really does interpret pain and it is not purely physical."

twenty two

Plasticity of the Brain

Studies in the 1990s discovered that our brain can adapt and change to form new pathways and frequencies. By changing our perspective of the pain we can change how it feels.[23]
learn more: http://amzn.to/1tSMVdB

twenty three

Subjective Pain

Studies have found that people can receive the same pain stimuli but their experience of the pain can be very different.[24]

learn more: http://amzn.to/1CKbfiC

twenty four

Open and Close the Gate

1965 research by Melzack and Wall created the Gate Control Theory. It stated that we have 'pain conducting neurons' which open the gate and 'pain inhibiting neurons' that close the gate. They concluded that any behaviour which creates pain inhibiting neurons, such as a mum kissing her child's wound better, or someone rubbing their arm better, prevents pain signals travelling to the brain. [25]
learn more: http://amzn.to/1CKbfiC

twenty five

Virtual World

An article published in the magazine 'Pain' states that a patient thought about their pain 95% of the time when playing a computer game, but only 2% of the time when he was immersed in a virtual reality experience.[26]
learn more: http://amzn.to/1CKbfiC

"Distraction is one of many powerful tools we can use to control pain."

Reason twenty six

Six Ds

Eimer and Freeman, in 1998, concluded that Deep Relaxation, Decatastrophizing, Direction, Distraction, Distortion and Dissociation are the six successful mind methods to manage pain.[27]
learn more: http://amzn.to/1rV63Vw

"Each one of these six methods has many techniques that can be learned to control our pain."

twenty seven

Meditation

A 2009 study by the University of North Carolina found that patients meditating for 20 minutes a day for 3 days, even if they had never meditated before, could change their perception to their pain.[28]
learn more: http://amzn.to/1CKbfiC

twenty eight

Love and Emotional Healing

Dr Andrew Weil states that he has seen many patients' back pain disappear when they fall in love or make big changes to their emotional outlook.[29]
learn more: http://amzn.to/1CKbfiC

twenty nine

Photo of a Loved One

A UCLA study in November 2009 discovered that simply by looking at a photograph of a loved one could reduce pain.[30]
learn more: http://amzn.to/1CKbfiC

Reason thirty

No More Pain

In 1997, a Bassman and Wester study developed the following acronym:

- **N**oticing where I am relatively comfortable
- **O**ptimising the control I have
- **M**otivating myself to engage in positive activities
- **O**pening my mind to new possibilities and choices (being flexible as much as possible)
- **R**elaxing in some regular way, e.g. using self-hypnosis regularly
- **E**valuating my time and priorities (Recall that managing chronic pain can be a full time job)
- **P**racticing self-hypnosis to gain some control over my pain and other symptoms
- **A**voiding stressful and conflictual situations as much as possible
- **I**ndividualizing my schedule and not being afraid to make "downtime" when the pain flares up
- **N**egotiating support from others[31]

learn more: http://amzn.to/1rV63Vw

Three Dimensions of Pain

Melzack and Casey developed three dimensions of pain. They are:

1. The Sensory
2. The Cognitive
3. The Motivation-Emotional[32]

learn more: http://amzn.to/1rV63Vw

"The great thing about these three dimensions is that they are all subjective and within your control, giving you influence over how much pain you feel."

Reason thirty two

Four A's of Pain Coping

A study by Brown and Fromm in 1987 concluded that people can use the following pain-coping strategies known as the Four A's: Avoidance, Alleviation, Alteration and Awareness.[33]
learn more: http://amzn.to/1rV63Vw

Worse Pain

Dabney Ewin discovered that because we can make our pain worse with our minds it proves that we can control the pain and therefore we must be able to reduce our pain too.[34]
learn more: http://amzn.to/1rV63Vw

Reason thirty four

Anyone Can Learn

Shinzen Young, a Buddhist practitioner, mindfulness master and pain management expert, states that with time, effort and determination we can learn to control pain and, once we get started and continue to practice, we can become good, just like practicing sports and music.[35]
learn more: http://amzn.to/1rVN8Lz

Burn Victims' Pain

When burn victims have their bandages changed it can be very painful. The University of Washington developed a virtual reality game called 'Snow World' immersing the individual in an icy-cool environment. This really helped soothe the pain, even more than Morphine.[36]

learn more: http://bit.ly/1FeoFSl

Reason thirty six

Methods to Control Pain

Milton Erickson categorised eleven methods of dealing with his own and his patients' pain.

1. Direct suggestion
2. Indirect suggestion
3. Create amnesia
4. Create numbness
5. Create distance
6. Alter sensations
7. Displace
8. Dissociation
9. Reinterpret
10. Distort time
11. Suggesting that the pain will reduce itself [37]

Noesitherapy

Dr. Ángel Escudero has performed over 10000 operations with a technique that is pure mind control. It involves producing and having saliva in your mouth and then directly suggesting a particular part of a body is numb.[38]
learn more: http://bit.ly/1uZ73Fp

thirty eight

Placebo Ranking

In 1957 Traut & Passarelli realised that to get greater results from a placebo it must be more believable and technically convincing. For example, placebo injections are more effective than placebo pills and placebo Morphine is more effective than placebo Aspirin.[39]
learn more: http://amzn.to/1s0ystC

thirty nine

Relativity of Pain

Pain Neurologist Arthur Craig has described how pain can be relative and emotional. He explains that if you get tackled to the ground in a family game of football it can be fun, yet exactly the same tackle whilst walking to work can hurt. Same damage, different pain.[40]

No Damage, High Pain

At the Barrow Neurological Institute neuro-scientist Arthur Craig created the 'Thermal Grill Illusion' a grill made from alternate hot and cold grill bars.

The experiment involved volunteers placing their hands on the grill. Amazingly it caused no damage, but it did cause excruciating pain.[41]

"This shows that pain is not created by damage but is registered by, and comes from, the brain."

forty one

Behaviour Therapy and Pain

Dr Tim Salomons from the University of Reading has discovered that participants given Cognitive Behaviour Therapy (CBT) to control negative thoughts prior to receiving heat pain had 38% less pain symptoms compared to the control group who were given no CBT.[42]

Reason forty two

Behavioural Change

Fordyce, in his 1973 and 1983 studies, concluded that those who comprehensively use cognitive behavioural programs for their pain generally learn to become more active, return to work, take less medication, and gain good function.[43]
learn more: http://amzn.to/1s0ystC

forty three

Angina Pain

In 1979 Benson and McCallie studied 13 types of medication, including a placebo, for treating heart pain. Of the 90 patients, 37% found the placebo the best for them. Out of the 13 drugs, the placebo was ranked fifth, beating 8 angina drugs on the market.[44]

learn more: http://amzn.to/1vHap2R

Reason forty four

Two Phases of Pain

Henry Beecher concluded that there are two phases to pain: the original 'Pain Sensation', i.e. actual injury; and, the 'Processing of Pain Sensation', i.e. our reaction, emotions, perceptions, etc.. [45]
learn more: http://amzn.to/1vHap2R

"By successfully dealing with the processing of the sensation, we can be left with discomfort of the actual injury, which is less than it was had we not dealt with the processing phase."

forty five

Multiply

According to the 1988 study by Price, expectation, clinical warmth, prestige and positive attitude will multiply the placebo analgesic response.[46]

Believe it Won't Work?

A 2011 study by the University of Oxford using brain imaging showed that if a patient did not believe in an effective pain medication the drug's chance of working was reduced or could be totally overridden.[47]

"Amazing! This shows the power of our expectations and beliefs."

Placebo is Real

A 2004 Columbia University study lead by Professor Wager showed that placebo is real. Using a brain scanner, the study concluded that the more the patient believed in the placebo, the less activity they had in the pain centre of their brain, thus reducing their overall pain.[48]

Reason forty eight

Vicious Cycle

Howard Schubiner MD states that there are three major parts of our nervous system that create the vicious cycle of pain:

1. The nerves that send pain signals from the body to the brain
2. The brain itself, where those nerve signals are interpreted
3. The nerves that send signals back to the body

He continues by saying we can, with a variety of techniques, retrain our brain to manage these three parts of the pain cycle.[49]

learn more: http://amzn.to/1tmKeju

Knitting the Pain Away

Since 2006, Betsan Corkhill has run a knitting group at the Pain Clinic at Royal United Hospital in Bath, UK, that doctors refer to as Knitting Therapy. In 2009, their research, along with the British Pain Society, found that knitting helps with pain because of the esteem it gives, the rhythmic movements, and the stimulation.[50]

Chapter two

50 Techniques to help you control pain with your mind.

The Muscle Technique

Starting from your head, working down to your feet, tense each and every muscle for a couple of seconds and then release them.[1]

learn more: http://amzn.to/ZKLS1q

one

The Control Centre

Picture yourself shrinking down into your body and going to your brain where you see a control centre with many dials and sliders. Find the dial or slider which is connected to your pain and discomfort. Before resetting the pain, note which number it is set to, one being the lowest and ten the highest. Now adjust the setting up one notch and notice the difference in sensation in your body, then start turning the setting down as far as you feel it can go.[2]
learn more: http://amzn.to/1whmOtB

two

Massage

A massage releases endorphins, our happy chemical, and helps lower pain. If you cannot have a massage, a self massage or hug while rubbing the side of your arms can help.[3]

three

Dr Weil's 4-7-8 Breathing Technique

- Exhale completely through your mouth, making a whoosh sound as you do.

- Close your mouth, then inhale quietly through your nose to a mental count of four.

- Hold your breath for a count of seven.

- Exhale completely through your mouth, making a whoosh sound to a count of eight.

This is one breath.

- Repeat the cycle three more times.[4]

learn more: http://amzn.to/1zgM0G6

Mantra

Sitting on a chair, take a few deep breaths. Repeat a mantra, which is best for you, over and over. If you prefer, writing it over and over again helps too.

An example of a mantra could be "I am in control of my pain and discomfort" or "Every day, hour, minute and second I am becoming more and more comfortable.".[5]
learn more: http://amzn.to/1whmOtB

five

Zoom Out

1. Make sure you are sitting or lying comfortably.
2. Recall the opening scene of an experience or memory of yourself in pain.
3. Zoom out until you see yourself within the scene, then zoom out even further so you can see the scene unfold as if you were a stranger that happened to pass by.
4. Play out the scene while maintaining the third-person perspective.
5. Make sure to employ a third person perspective whenever you find yourself reflecting on the experience.[6]

learn more: http://amzn.to/1uoxHYf

Mist

Imagine the painful area of your body being filled with a cooling, luminous mist that dissolves all negative sensations. If properly convinced, your brain should eliminate the feeling of pain.[7]

seven

Timeline

In your mind, imagine a timeline stretching out from both sides of your head: one side representing the past and the other side the future. Now picture a time in the past when you were not in pain and mentally put yourself back in your body at that time to note the sensation.[8]
learn more: http://amzn.to/ZAQzL0

Rocking

Breathing and rocking can be a great way to relieve discomfort. Rocking back and forth on each breath is very helpful. If you are able, cross your arms across your chest and stroke the sides of your upper arms to add to the relieving of discomfort.[9]

Technique nine

Soaking in the Tub

Relaxation can make a great difference to pain, so a long relaxing bath can be very helpful. Focusing on the sensation of the water on your skin or the scent of the bath fragrance also helps.[10]

Avoidance

Our conscious mind can only focus on one thing at a time. Putting all your attention on one task can make a big difference. One such task could be focusing on washing up the dishes with such care and attention as if you were bathing the baby Jesus, baby Buddha, or the most precious thing you can think of.[11]

learn more: http://amzn.to/1whmOtB

Technique eleven

Noesitherapy

This method is surprisingly effective at reducing and numbing sensations. The key is keeping your mouth full of saliva and focusing on the part of the body you numb, e.g. the right arm. Say and repeat to yourself 3 times, with the saliva in your mouth;

"My Right Arm [or any other part of your body] is completely psychologically anaesthetised"[12]
learn more: http://amzn.to/1tCUvsl

twelve

Altered Focus

Choose a part of your body not experiencing pain and focus your attention on that part to increase the temperature. Really concentrate and work to up the heat of that area of your body.[13]

"You can even test this with a thermometer to see the before and after temperature"

Dissociation

Visualise a journey to your favourite place in the world, or tour around the universe. Visit people, alive or not, and have conversations you would love to have or have had.[14]
learn more: http://amzn.to/1whmOtB

"In your mind there is a world where anything is possible!"

Technique fourteen

Sensory Splitting

Focus on all the different sensations you feel within the pain. The sensations could be hot, sharp, pins and needles, stiff, hard, or any other sensation. Then, pick one sensation and focus all your attention on changing it. For example, if it is hot, focus on cooling it, or if it is sharp, focus and concentrate on blunting it.[15]

Technique fifteen

Mental Anaesthesia

This can be very powerful, just close your eyes and imagine having an anaesthetic injection into the painful area and numbing it. Really picture it happening. [16]

sixteen

Mental Analgesia

Imagine taking a pain-killing tablet, rubbing on pain gel, or having a morphine injection to relieve the pain. Imagine and feel the pain-reducing substance working the area and reducing the discomfort.[17]

seventeen

Transfer

Note a part of your body which is not in pain and magnify this feeling. When ready, move it to the area of pain or discomfort to help reduce or remove the pain.[18]

Age Progression

Picture a time in the future, or even the past, when you feel no pain. Picture yourself and notice the sensations you are feeling. Then, when ready, bring those sensations and feelings into the now for you to feel.[19]

nineteen

Symbolic Imagery

Find something that you feel symbolises your pain. This may be an animal, light, a vehicle or noise. Work on changing that symbol to reflect less discomfort: if it is light, dim the brightness; if it is a loud noise, turn down the volume. Note how the pain becomes less.[20]

Positive Imagery

Think of your safest, happiest and most relaxing place. Picture every detail of yourself there and immerse yourself in this place - sights, sounds, smells and emotions.[21]

twenty one

Counting

Count anything you wish, for example, the number of sheep in the field, the breaths that you take in a minute, or blades of grass in a small square. Whatever you choose to count, calmly make it your goal to find the answer by focusing on the task.[22]

Move the Pain

Picture the pain in one area of the body, then with your imagination move the pain to another part of your body - perhaps to your hand, where you can more easily manage it by rubbing it, warming it up, cooling it down, waving it around, or whatever will help gain more comfort.[23]

twenty three

Your Present Moment

Describe everything you are experiencing in the present moment, without anxieties about the past or worries about the future. Focus solely on the concrete description in the now, like "I am sitting in this chair with my feet on the ground, wearing a red jumper in discomfort".

Keep away from emotional descriptors such as "excruciating", "frustrated", "angry", etc. - they only confuse this exercise. Just concentrate and become aware of what you are doing now that can be seen.[24]

learn more: http://amzn.to/1yOPTB0

"By accepting where you are right now, you have the foundations to change and build the next moment upon."

Technique twenty four

Body Scan

Take a few deep breaths to relax and then start by taking your attention and breath to the thumb on the right hand. Work your way along your hand, up your arm, around your shoulder, down your back on the right side, down your right leg and foot, taking your breath and attention to each part as you go. Repeat on the left side before focusing on your neck and around the parts of your head. If you discover any tension or discomfort, focus your breath and love on the area, then continue on with the body scan until you have finished.[25]

learn more: http://amzn.to/1yOPTB0

Technique twenty five

Meditation

Sit in a comfortable position and take a few deep breaths in and out, with no emotional reaction or attachment to the pain. Be aware of its sensation. Don't try and push it away, just sit with the pain and realise that at the moment it is part of you, but with no emotional reaction within. You are just sitting, breathing and being with the pain in acceptance - you may even want to dance with the pain.[26]
learn more: http://amzn.to/1zgMgow

"Like any conflict, it is generally resolved by talking and even friendship."

Technique twenty six

Change the Number

On a scale of 1-10, with ten the highest score for your pain, visualise your pain as that number. See that number and be aware of it as a representation of your pain. Notice for just one second as the number goes up by one, how the pain increases. Now notice as the number slowly drops down, a digit at a time, until it reaches a number you feel comfortable with.[27]

learn more: http://amzn.to/1wdmQDN

Technique twenty seven

Bucket of Ice Water

Visualise a big freezing cold bucket of water ready for you to lower your hand into. Starting with the fingertips, slowly imagine submerging the whole hand up to the wrist. Feeling the ice cold water all the way around the hand, imagine the cold engulf the hand until it goes numb. When it does, with your mind transfer the numbness to the part of your body in discomfort.[28]
learn more: http://amzn.to/1wdmQDN

twenty eight

Exciting or Scared

Focus on something that scares you or excites you. Picture every detail and sensation you may feel. Perhaps a lion is about to attack, or you are on a fairground ride and you are looking over the edge of a big dip, or perhaps you are even about to do your first parachute jump.[29]

"Your mind will more than likely take the excited or scared feeling above the pain or discomfort."

twenty nine

Laughter

Watch a funny film or your favourite comedian. Laughing helps your body release its natural painkillers (endorphins).[30]

Exercise

Practicing light forms of exercise, like Yoga or Tai Chi, can help keep you flexible and loose to enable your outer body, as well as your inner body, to flow and move. This also produces endorphins, known to be a natural painkiller.[31]

thirty one

Leave Your Body Behind

Sit or lie down with no distractions. Imagine yourself leaving your body and going somewhere a long way away to do an activity which you find very engrossing and absorbing. This could be any activity on any planet. Take your time to explore freely without your body.[32]
learn more: http://amzn.to/1tCUVzh

thirty two

Distraction

Using your thumb and forefinger on one hand, pinch the webbing between the thumb and forefinger on the other. First notice the pain, then notice all the different types of sensations you can feel as you press.[33]
learn more: http://amzn.to/1whmOtB

"There are many other forms of distraction that work, like having a conversation, getting engrossed in TV, film, a jigsaw or computer game."

thirty three

Dissolve Pain

Taking a few deep breaths, close your eyes and become aware of yourself sat in the room. Then imagine feeling the space that your whole body occupies, imagine feeling the space between the center of the pain or discomfort you feel and the back of your body and finally imagine feeling the space between your thumb and forefinger. Really visualise that space and its feeling before opening your eyes.[34]

learn more: http://amzn.to/1qTL2X7

thirty four

Distance

Picture yourself getting on a train for a long journey home. As you board, you leave your pain on the station platform. As the train pulls away, look back, seeing the pain getting further and further away. As you do this you may begin to notice the changes in your body - as you continue down the track you can no longer see the pain. As you make your journey home, note that each second you are moving further away from the pain and discomfort but closer and closer to your home of comfort.[35]

learn more: http://amzn.to/1uozrkc

Technique thirty five

Distortion

With your imagination take your pain out of your body and hold it in your hands. Note its colour, size, shape, weight and texture. Then, with your mind, mould and sculpt this object into one which represents comfort and place it back in your body.[36]
learn more: http://amzn.to/1whmOtB

thirty six

Direct Suggestion

Repeat to yourself "I am not in pain, because I choose not to be right now.", "I am not in pain, because I choose not to be right now.", "I am not in pain, because I choose not to be right now."[37]

"Simple, but can be very effective, just like Noesitherapy."

thirty seven

Dimmer Switch

In your mind, imagine walking into a room. Turning the dimmer switch to light up the room, you notice that as the room gets lighter your discomfort and pain becomes less. You are seeing the light. Now play with the dimmer switch to find the best setting for you right now.[38]
learn more: http://amzn.to/1whmOtB

You In Wonderland

In this Wonderland, you, like Alice, can grow and shrink at will - as you imagine getting bigger and smaller, notice how this changes the discomfort and pain. Does your pain increase or decrease as you get bigger? So, when you get smaller, the opposite is true, isn't that so? Give it a go and find out.[39]

Technique thirty nine

Number Blackboard

Visualise a blackboard - the number you see being written represents your current level of discomfort. Knowing that the blackboard shows your pain score, you can now erase the number and instruct or write for yourself the number you would like, going down in increments until you get to the most comfortable sensation for you.[40]
learn more: http://amzn.to/1whmOtB

Glove Anaesthesia

Close your eyes and take a few deep breaths. Imagine going outside on a really cold, snowy day. You are all wrapped up warm except for one of your hands, which is not covered. Feel the cold air on the hand and notice as you pick up the snow and throw snowballs how much colder that hand is getting. Keep playing in the cold, icy snow until your hand goes numb. With your awareness of your numb hand, if you can reach, place your numb hand on the part of your body in discomfort and transfer the numbness into that area, focusing on how comfortable and numb that area becomes.[41]

learn more: http://amzn.to/1ylmlrL

Technique forty one

Make Friends

Start an inner discussion with your discomfort and pain. Listen to what it has to say. Hear why the pain and discomfort is there and in what way it feels it is benefiting you. Share your feelings and story regarding the discomfort, explain how it effects your life and what you would like to change.[42]
learn more: http://amzn.to/1whmOtB

"It sounds odd, but dialogue always precedes the end of war, a compromise could be had, and then friendship."

Technique forty two

Reject Unnecessary Pain

Take a few deep breaths and get close to your pain by looking, listening and feeling it. Investigate the sensations and imagine all the nerve signals travelling up and down the spine from the discomfort to the brain. Now ask yourself, and let your inner mind tell you, how many of those travelling signals to the brain are really needed. Maybe some are, however, maybe none are required - just let your inner being set the correct amount of sensations.[43]
learn more: http://amzn.to/1whmOtB

forty three

Decatastrophizing

Catch your thoughts about your pain, note if they are negative or positive. If they are negative, flip them to the polar opposite, then find the middle ground between the two. Do this for each thought you catch.[44]

learn more: http://amzn.to/1whmOtB

"By watching our thoughts and feelings and flipping them, it helps us control our emotional reaction and therefore reduces the sensations."

forty four

Prepare Yourself

When you notice the pain arising, try saying to yourself - "I'm going to get ready to deal with this. I can handle this. I have coped with this before. This time it will be easier for me to manage. I will be okay. I can listen to what my body is telling me. I can learn something from this. It's a shame to waste 'good pain'."[45]

learn more: http://amzn.to/1whmOtB

"Preparing is step one of four from Bruce Eimer's Stress Inoculation Training - the others focus on 'during', 'the worst moments' and 'after' the pain."

Technique forty five

Clenched Fist

Focus on one of your hands, putting all your attention on it. As you breathe in clench your fist, feel the tension, and then clench it even harder. Hold that fist and your breath for a few seconds, being aware of the tense sensation. As you breathe out, release the fist, shake out your hand and become aware of the release of tension.[46]

learn more: http://amzn.to/1whmOtB

"This is a quicker and simpler version of the Progressive Muscle Technique."

Technique forty six

Shadow

Picture a lovely sunny day and as the sun shines you notice your shadow - wherever you go this shadow follows. With your mind, move your discomfort or pain into the shadow and let it follow you as you go about. Notice how you feel as the sun goes behind a cloud and your shadow fades.[47]
learn more: http://amzn.to/1whmOtB

forty seven

Lock it Away

Close your eyes, take a few deep breaths, and imagine finding your discomfort or pain. Move it from your body to the other side of the room and ask it to stay there while you do what you need to do. Then, go out and do what you need to do, not forgetting to lock it up before you leave.[48]

learn more: http://amzn.to/1whmOtB

forty eight

Breaking the Pain Apart

As you feel the pain, accept it, then move it away from you. Imagine the pain shattering into a thousand pieces. Now just focus on one of those tiny little pieces, feel the sensation of only that little piece.[49]

learn more: http://bit.ly/TimCridland

"This amazing technique is one of the favourites used by Tim Cridland - an expert at controlling pain."

Technique forty nine

Finger Rubbing

Should you feel discomfort rising, start rubbing your thumb and forefinger together, really focusing on the sensation, texture, temperature and any other feelings.[50]
learn more: http://amzn.to/1whmOtB

Chapter three

50 Examples of people healing their body with their mind.

Knee Operation

A 2002 study looked at knee surgery and its effectiveness. The study had 3 groups:

1. Had the operation to remove damaged cartilage.
2. Had their knee joint cleaned.
3. Had fake surgery - knee cut open nothing done then sewed back up.

All 3 groups had the same aftercare and, more importantly, recovered and improved in their mobility to equal levels.[1]

"This shows to me that the mind can heal the body with belief."

Example one

Wart-Ever You Think

Under hypnosis, 14 people covered in warts were told that one side of their body would be free of warts. A couple of weeks later almost all the warts had gone on that side of the patient's body.[2]
learn more: http://amzn.to/1s9r0x7

"This makes me wonder what else in and on the human body can be controlled by the human mind."

Ice Water

Alberto Villoldo from San Francisco State College asked people to place one arm in ice water. He found that the group which had practiced meditation and self healing visualisations could deal with the pain better and, even more interestingly, two-thirds of this group could, after a precautionary post-study blood test, stop their bleeding by thought alone.[3]

"In my opinion, meditation and visualisation can take our brain and body to next level."

three

Pacemaker

In 1999 a Swedish hospital fitted 80 heart patients with a pacemaker to help with their condition. However, they only switched on 40 of the 80 pacemakers. The results after 3 months were that both groups stated they felt better and had increased use of the heart.[4]

"A main organ of the body improved by a belief that the pacemaker was helping. The mind is amazing."

Example four

Fighting Spirit

A King's College study explored the views and beliefs of breast cancer patients 3 months after their mastectomy. Patients who had a fighting spirit, denial or acceptance had, after 5 and 10 years, a much higher rate of survival than those who felt hopeless and helpless.[5]

"This helps me cement my view that by changing our attitude we have a positive effect on our body."

Maids Lose Weight

Hotel maids work physically hard and, in theory, they should be burning lots of calories and be fit. However, this is not always case, so Ellen Langer of Harvard decided to split a group of maids into two groups. One group was told they were doing more exercise than was expected in one day. One month later, the researchers found that the group with the exercise information had lost more weight and lower blood pressure than the group without the information.[6]

learn more: http://amzn.to/10Giv10

"All that changed was perception - if you change your perception what else could you change?"

Heart and the Canoe

A patient with blocked arteries, after every other option was tried, was told by his doctor to visualise. For 20 minutes each day the patient imagined he was paddling through his arteries scraping and clearing any blockages. After a couple of months the x-rays showed his arteries were much clearer, and he was no longer needing his wheelchair.[7]

"Visualisation is good enough to improve performance in Olympians, so why not for us and our health?"

Delaying Death

A New York Hospice, for the first time in its history, recorded no deaths in the month of December 1999. With everything going back to normal in January 2000, they realised the patients really wanted to see the new Millennium, so held on.[8]

"We can't put death off forever, however, it seems our mental attitude can have some say over when."

Example eight

Breast Cancer Recovery

A study by Belgian Professor Fabienne Roelants found that patients undergoing breast cancer surgery recovered more quickly if they had hypnosis and local anaesthetic. Each patient needed less painkillers and left hospital a day earlier than those who had the same operation with general anaesthetic.[9]

Being Positive

A study by Duke University Medical Center in 2003 found, after examining 866 patients with heart conditions, that patients who generally felt more positive emotions were 20% more likely to be alive in 11 years in comparison to those who experienced negative emotions on regular basis.[10]
learn more: http://amzn.to/10Giv10

"This is amazing because there are many techniques we can use to give us positive feelings and, therefore, increase our chances of living longer."

Example ten

Breathe Mindfully

In a study of 40 people with asthma, each was given an inhaler which contained nothing but water vapour, however they were told it contained a drug that would tighten the airways. 19 of the 40 people experienced breathing difficulties and of the 19, 12 experienced an asthma attack. These 19 were then given the same water vapor but this time were told it would help their symptoms and it did.[11]
learn more: http://amzn.to/10Giv10

"Just through suggestion alone an asthma attack can appear, so why not suggest to ourselves daily that we intend to get well quicker?"

Example eleven

An Injection of Belief

A 1954 study of patients with bleeding ulcers gave half the group an injection that they were told was a drug that would cure them. The other half were given an injection but were told that it may or may not cure them. Both groups were in fact given water injections, however 70% of the 'cure' group improved, compared to 25% of the 'maybe' group.[12]

learn more: http://amzn.to/10Giv10

"This suggests to me that exploring and challenging our beliefs can help our recovery."

Example twelve

Placebo & Nocebo

An Ohio University study found that when a positive outcome of better sleep was suggested, optimists responded better. When a negative outcome of feeling unwell was suggested, pessimist responded better. All from a pill with no medical value.[13]
learn more: http://amzn.to/10Giv10

Example thirteen

Imagine That!

A 2003 study by the Karolinsha Institute in Stockholm proved that when we imagine moving our fingers, toes or tongue, it activates the same part of the brain as when we actually move that body part.[14]
learn more: http://amzn.to/10Giv10

"This study reminds me of the scene from the Quentin Tarantino film 'Kill Bill' when the main character successfully encourages herself to wiggle her toe."

Example fourteen

Imagine Yourself Stronger

The Lerner Research Institute split 30 volunteers into two groups. One group was given a little finger exercise for 15 minutes a day. The second group was asked to do the same exercise but to only use their minds. The results after 12 weeks were; the little fingers' strength improved by 53% for the exercise group, compared to an amazing 35% for those who only used their mind.[15]

learn more: http://amzn.to/10Giv10

"Arnold Schwarzenegger imagined his biceps 'as big as mountain peaks' as he did curling exercises, it seems to have worked for him."

Example fifteen

Be Your Guide

Of 24 patients who had gallbladder operations, the people who used Guided Imagery all healed their wounds quicker and therefore recovered faster. This study was carried out by Southeastern Louisiana University.[16]

learn more: http://amzn.to/10Giv10

"Guided Imagery is a directed form of visualisation to lead imagination to an individual's goal."

Example sixteen

Visualisation & Physiotherapy

A 2007 study by the University of Cincinnati looked at the power of visualisation. It found that, out of the 32 patients involved, the 16 in the group that received visualisation alongside their physiotherapy had more movement that the other group of 16 that only received physiotherapy.[17]
learn more: http://amzn.to/10Giv10

"Visualisation can enable us to focus on our goal and the best possible outcome."

Example seventeen

Brain Training to Move

A study published in 'Experimental Brain Research' showed that tetraplegics and paraplegics who were taught visualisation to imagine moving their tongue and feet actually developed more movement in their tongue and feet.[18]
learn more: http://amzn.to/10Giv10

"The more we look around, we can find many examples of how we can extend our achievements using the power of our minds."

Example eighteen

Stressing the Point

In 2004 data was collated from 293 studies and stated that stress makes our immune system's ability to fight off illness a lot less effective than when we are calm.[19]
learn more: http://amzn.to/10Giv10

"Wow, just by learning to deal with our stress and learning to be calm we can increase our chance of recovery."

Being Proud & Assertive

A study of people diagnosed with tumors found that the tumors were thinner in those who were co-operative, assertive and expressing their emotions.[20]
learn more: http://amzn.to/10Giv10

"Deep down we all know what is best for ourselves and if we can learn how to express positive feelings and thoughts we can become healthier."

Example twenty

Don't Catch Colds

A 2003 study by Carnegie Mellon University found that, when introduced to a cold virus, people who were generally positive in the beginning were less like to catch it.[21]

learn more: http://amzn.to/10Gjkai

"We can learn how to be more positive and mindful, which means we can control another element of our health."

twenty one

Going to be Sick?

One study gave a 'vomiting liquid' to a group of patients - 80% were sick, even though it was just sweetened water.[22]

learn more: http://amzn.to/10Gjkai

"Amazing, this shows the power of our belief to affect our body. It's fantastic that we can change and develop our thoughts and beliefs, meaning we can control our body and health."

Example twenty two

Chapter 3 - 50 Examples of people healing their body with their mind.

The Power of Belief

A study by The British Stomach Cancer Group found that 30% percent of a Placebo group lost their hair and 56% were sick when taking nothing more than a sugar pill.[23]
learn more: http://amzn.to/10Gjkai

"The power of belief and expectation is very fascinating. It makes me wonder what else belief can do."

twenty three

Laugh Yourself Better

A study performed in California shows that laughter and watching a funny film increase the cells which help your immune system. The cells are the virus-fighting T-cells and Natural Killer (NK) cells.[24]
learn more: http://amzn.to/10Gjkai

"So, next time you are poorly, perhaps your favourite funny film could help you recover quicker."

twenty four

The Social Network

Of the 276 people involved in a 1997 Carnegie Mellon University study, it was found that those who were more sociable and had more friends were 20% better at fighting off a cold.[25]
learn more: http://amzn.to/10Gjkai

"This study helps us understand why visitors to patients in hospitals help so much."

Example twenty five

Stress Test

A Harvard Medical School study helped conclude that being unable to deal with stress is one the most detrimental things that can happen to our immune system. This is because it affects the NK Cells which are very good at attacking viruses and cancer cells.[26]
learn more: http://amzn.to/10Gjkai

"There are many ways we can learn to deal with stress - one effective way is meditation."

twenty six

Positivity and Cancer

The American Psychosomatic Society in a 1995 study discovered cancer was less likely to recur in people who are optimistic.[27]
learn more: http://amzn.to/10Gjkai

"It doesn't matter how thin you slice something, it always has two sides. What is the good side of a bad situation?"

Example twenty seven

Live Long and Prosper

Harvard University research found that optimistic men had better health and were more likely to be alive 20-35 years later.[28]
learn more: http://amzn.to/10Gjkai

"Which affirmations could you use to help train your mind to be positive on certain issues?"

twenty eight

Stroke

A study in the journal 'Stroke' indicated that stroke victims who felt helpless and hopeless died sooner than those who are positive and hopeful.[29]
learn more: http://amzn.to/10Gjkai

"Same illness, but a different outlook - as humans we have the power to change our perspective to increase our chance of living longer. We are truly amazing."

Liver or Die

A patient was told, as recalled in the Southern Medical Journal, that his cancer had spread to his liver and that he was not long for this world. A few months later he passed away, only for his autopsy to show a misdiagnosis. It was stated that he died from fear.[30]

learn more: http://amzn.to/10Gjkai

"Louise L Hay has called fear 'False Evidence Appearing Real', as we know our brain cannot tell the difference between imagined and real actions."

Example thirty

Your Guide

The Cleveland Clinic Foundation's 1997 study found that a patient who listened to relaxation and guided imagery tapes before their major bowel surgery had less pain, less stress, took less medication, and recovered quicker.[31]

learn more: http://amzn.to/10Gjkai

"This simple act could save so much money for the Health Service, I wonder why we do not do this more."

thirty one

Angry Man

Angry bi-sexual and gay men with HIV tended to have less T-cells which help the immune system in comparison with bi-sexual and gay men with HIV who were calmer.[32]
learn more: http://amzn.to/10Gjkai

Guilty as Charged

Hull University asked students to state their favourite activities and rate them for pleasure and guilt. When saliva samples were taken, the students with high guilt ratings had lower levels of the body's natural antibody than those with lower guilt ratings.[33]
learn more: http://amzn.to/10Gjkai

thirty three

Immunity Focus

Karen Olness and colleagues clearly demonstrated that subjects could increase white blood cells called 'Neutrophils', which help defend the body against infection. They did this with imagination alone.[34]

learn more: http://amzn.to/10Gjkai

Example thirty four

Wheezy Does It

A 2005 study published in the Proceedings of the National Academy of Science showed patients with Asthma could have an attack just by hearing stressful words like 'wheeze'.[35]
learn more: http://amzn.to/10Gjkai

thirty five

Feedback

Under the guidance of Dr Steven Fahrion, his patient learned that by using his imagination he could warm up a chosen hand with just the power of his mind.[36]
learn more: http://amzn.to/1vIIL45

"Biofeedback shows and charts changes in the body's response. It is a fantastic way of showing how the mind affects the body."

thirty six

Spontaneous Remissions

Erik Peper, Ph.D student at Harvard, reported on all the cases of spontaneous remissions from cancer. The repeating factor throughout the recoveries was that the individuals took responsibility for their body and health. They developed an attitude of hope, effort, determination and positivity.[37]
learn more: http://amzn.to/1vIIL45

"The Silva Method states that to make positive Mind-Body changes, a person needs desire, belief and expectancy that the event will occur."

thirty seven

The Wonder Drug?

A bedridden patient with severe terminal cancer had heard of a new drug called Kerbiozen. He begged, and eventually persuaded, his doctor to prescribe it to him. Within a few days he was, amazingly, up and about, and his scans showed his cancer had shrunk. He was great until he read that the drug test for Kerbiozen had not been successful, and returned to his bedridden state.[38]
learn more: http://amzn.to/1vIIL45

"The power of Placebo and belief. I hope, like me, you are now beginning to see the power of our minds."

Example thirty eight

The New Wonder Drug?

The doctor of the 'Kerbiozen patient' thought he would try a Placebo test, telling and giving the patient the new 'stronger' version of Kerbiozen. Again he recovered, with his cancer shrinking away once more, until he read the final Kerbiozen Government report stating its failure rate. The patient passed away shortly after.[39]

learn more: http://amzn.to/1vIIL45

"Truly amazing, and would suggest that like the wart experiment (see #2) our mind can control our bodies in many, many ways."

Whatever You Think

Dr. Elmer Green of the Menninger Foundation stated that if studies prove that we can make ourselves ill with our minds, then it goes without saying that we can make ourselves better with our minds too.[40]
learn more: http://amzn.to/1vIIL45

"I, for one, feel this is true, because the more studies I read, the more I am sure that our mind has the ability to make us both poorly and well."

Example forty

Make a Difference

A 2008 study suggested that 90-95% of all cancer is caused by lifestyle or environmental factors. Factors which include cigarette smoking, diet, alcohol, sun exposure, environmental pollutants, infections, stress, obesity, and physical inactivity.[41]

"This study shows we have many ways to control our health. The choices we make about our lifestyle and how we choose to manage any stresses can have a huge difference on the illnesses we may get and how we recover from it."

forty one

Seeing Multiple Personalities

Dr. Braun, a specialist in treating multiple personalities at the Rush-Presbyterian-St. Luke's Medical Center in Chicago, reports that many of his patients have several different spectacles, one for each personality because their vision changes along with their persona.[42]

"Truly amazing and, I feel, very strong proof that it is the mind that controls illness and the body as a whole."

forty two

Adult or Child Mind

An American Psychiatric Press article states how a doctor noticed that the same tranquilising drug had completely different effects on the same person, depending whether the person was in their Adult or Child persona.[43]

"Same drug, same person, different mindset producing a different result. The brain clearly has a massive influence over the body."

forty three

Poison Ivy

A 1984 study tested a famous 1962 experiment with people who were allergic to Poison Ivy. The participants were touched on the arm with Poison Ivy, this normally brings them out in a rash. They were told, however, that they were just harmless leaves. Only 1 in 5 reacted to the Poison Ivy, and when Hypnosis was used it was 1 in 8.[44]
learn more: http://amzn.to/1rdO4Vc

"The brain believed the suggestion, so the body did not react to the Poison Ivy."

Example forty four

Princeton Students

Princeton students threw a party but told none of the guests that they had replaced the beer in the keg with a beer that was 0.4% and virtually impossible to get drunk on. The results were that the student still behaved in a very drunk way, slurring their words and sleeping on the floor.[45]

"The power of belief made them think they were drunk."

forty five

Which Doctor is Correct?

New Scientist published a story about a man (Vance) who had met up with a witch doctor who told him he would die. Within weeks Vance was very ill, though medical doctors could find nothing physically wrong him. When a doctor found out from the victim's wife what had happened, the doctor developed a story and convinced Vance that he'd met the witch doctor and sorted everything for him. Vance made a full recovery very soon after.[46]

Example forty six

Cancer Be Gone

David Seidler, the writer of 'The King's Speech', tells of how he felt he had nothing to lose by trying to imagine his bladder cancer away. He did this for the two weeks leading up to his operation. At the pre-op biopsy they could find very little sign of any cancer. [47]

"There are lots of stories of how people who tell of how they imagined their cancer away."

Suicide Attempt

A patient tried to take his own life by taking 26 antidepressants which, unbeknown to him, were Placebo pills. Even so, his blood pressure dropped dangerously low and he required treatment.[48]

"Placebo are supposed to have a positive outcome to your body, where as Nocebo suggest a negative outcome."

forty eight

Hypno-Band

A lady lost 55lb using hypnosis. She was encouraged to believe she'd had gastric band surgery, thus reducing the amount of food her stomach could take at one time.[49]

"If you can lose weight through hypnotic gastric band surgery, I wonder what other hypno suggestive surgery could help us with in our lives."

Blistered

Under hypnosis, it was suggested that the normal pen touching the client's arm was a red hot poker. The client, believing this, then blistered where the pen had touched their skin.[50]
learn more: http://amzn.to/1s4ndkQ

"This is similar and reminds me of the Poison Ivy Experiment (see #44)."

Chapter four

50 Techniques to help the body recover using the mind.

Imagine the Growth Melting

Picture your growth or tumor just melting away. You could visualise a mini you shrinking down, going into your body, and melting it with a blow torch, or you could instruct your body to heat it up and melt it away.[1]

learn more: http://amzn.to/13KZM5q

Weaving the Marrow

For broken bones, close your eyes and breathe out 3 times. Imagine the two ends of the bones touching and the marrow flowing from one part into the other. As the marrow flows back and forth between the two parts, become aware of how each part of the bone is getting closer and closer together. See the two ends knitting together, getting stronger and stronger as this marrow knits together.[2]

learn more: http://amzn.to/13WBWnR

"This is clearly instructing your body with what you would like it to do."

Technique two

Helter-Skelter

Imagine yourself shrinking right down and entering your body somewhere in your head. Then slide yourself down a fun, swirly helter-skelter to the part of the body you would like to work on. When you arrive find a comfortable place to sit and instruct the cells of this area of the body to do exactly what you would like them to do.[3]

learn more: http://amzn.to/1Ael5rP

three

Blood Flow

Close your eyes and take a few deep breaths. Take your focus to your heart and imagine all the blood flowing around your body. As it does, notice all the nutrients you need to live are being transported to where it is needed. Imagine a vehicle picking up the nutrients and needs for the part of your body that you would like to recover. Once full, deliver it to this part of your body and notice how it improves and changes.[4]

learn more: http://amzn.to/1vJg86q

"Dr. Parkyn[4] comments: "No organ of the body can perform its functions properly when the amount of blood supplied to it is insufficient.""

Technique four

Popping Balloons

Picture the ill or unhealthy cells as balloons and imagine them being popped and disappearing.[5]
learn more: http://amzn.to/1Ael5rP

"This is a very powerful meditation as each time you do it you can feel that there is less and less illness in your body."

Technique five

Plump Healthy Cells

Imagine your healthy cells as plump and juicy berries and your unhealthy cells as dried, wrinkled and shrivelled pieces of fruit. You can imagine a bird acting as the immune system, flying in and taking the unhealthy cells away from your body. Alternatively you can picture the unhealthy cells being watered, back to healthy, productive and good cells that work for your body by blossoming into plump healthy cells.[6]
learn more: http://amzn.to/1BodqGR

Affirmations

"In every way I am getting better and better." is one affirmation that can be repeated over and over each day.

You can repeat this until your body understands this is what you would like it to do and you believe this is what is happening.[7]
learn more: http://amzn.to/1Ael5rP

seven

Intention

If we intend to do something we generally do it, because we put our focus on it. So, it is worth repeatedly affirming to yourself: "I intend to recover", "I intend to get over this condition", or whatever works for you, always beginning with "I intend...".[8]
learn more: http://amzn.to/13WBWnR

Technique eight

Shower in Pure Health

Whilst standing in a shower, imagine the water entering your body at the crown of your head and flushing any illness through your body, out of your toes, and down the plug hole.[9]

learn more: http://amzn.to/1Ael5rP

Ideal Scene

In your mind's eye, picture your perfect scene of exactly how you would like everything to be. Imagine yourself now stepping into this scene, and your body within this scene. Take note of all your feelings and senses. Say to yourself "I don't know how this is going to happen, I just know that it is so, Now!", then send it out into the universe to make it happen, trusting that it will. [10]

learn more: http://amzn.to/1rEuRmH

Technique ten

Laser Eyes

Shrink down and imagine finding the rogue agents in your body, eliminating them with lasers from your laser eyes until it is all gone. "Zap Zap" them with your eyes as you spot any rogue agents invading! Keep doing this until the area is given the all clear.[11]

learn more: http://amzn.to/1Ael5rP

Magic Eraser

On a piece of paper, with your body shape drawn on it draw in pencil the object or growth on the paper which represents its position in your body. Then, carefully and mindfully, happily remove it with an eraser. You could also say to yourself, or out loud, as you are doing this: "I erase this growth on this piece of paper. I erase this growth from my body.".[12]

twelve

The Workforce

Imagine yourself shrinking down, going into your body with a team of workers working just for you. As you go to the part of the body that you would like to recover, you can give your team instructions to repair this situation. Then, throughout the day, you can check back in with your workforce to see how they are getting on, to see if they are meeting the targets or even surpassing them![13]
learn more: http://amzn.to/1Ael5rP

thirteen

Crossroads

Relax and imagine yourself standing at a crossroads, notice how each road goes in a different direction further and further from each other. Each road has a curve taking the rest of the road out of sight. Place any desires behind one of the bends and behind another road's bend, place your fears. Examine the road with your desires. What does it look like? What are the surroundings like? What else is created from your mind? Then, do the same for the road which has your fears hidden around the bend. Going back or straight on at this crossroad keeps everything the same, but choosing to head down one of the other roads away from your desires or fears is now your choice.[14]

learn more: http://amzn.to/1L7Bt3D

Soldiers

Picture your immune system as an army with an ever-growing number of soldiers heading towards the area you wish to recover and heal. When they arrive, note how they take care of the enemy. They may eliminate them or escort them out of the body, never to be seen again, whichever suits you the best.[15]

learn more: http://amzn.to/1Ael5rP

Body Scan

In a comfortable place, take a few deep relaxing breaths. As you take a breath take your awareness to a different part of your body, starting at the top of your head and working down to your feet on the right-hand side of your body, then do the same on your left: top of my head, my right ear, my right cheek, right nostril, and so on. If you spot anywhere that has tension or pain, just give that area permission to relax and move on to the next part of your body. At the end, if you want to give a specific instruction for a certain part of your body to recover, you can do this by repeating it with loving kindness three times.[16]

learn more: http://amzn.to/1GRtsQK

Ask your Doctor & Imagine Recovery

Find out from your doctor exactly what would need to happen for you to make a full recovery. Once you know, picture this happening inside your body. Imagine it over and over again.[17]
learn more: http://amzn.to/13KZM5q

seventeen

Building Repairs

Imagine a workforce of builders working to join both parts of the bone back together. Setting up their scaffolding, attaching the two pieces together, building up around it to make it stronger, and finally finishing it off with a good strong layer of plaster on the outside to make the bone as good as new.[18]

learn more: http://amzn.to/1Ael5rP

Technique eighteen

Mind Mirror

Closing your eyes, imagine a full length mirror and in that mirror see a reflection of yourself with your current health condition. Become aware of your expressions, posture and actions. Note your attitude and feelings around your health. Observe all you can about this reflection. Now, with a deep breath in, erase the problem you are having - make it just disappear. Look at yourself again, free from the issue, and once again note your expression, posture, action and attitude. At this point, increase your desire for this reflection to become true by saying "This is who I am and how I am going to be, now.".[19]

learn more: http://amzn.to/1L7Bt3D

Ask the Illness

If there is part of your body that is poorly, calm yourself and ask that part of the body if it has a message for you. Perhaps ask what is the best thing you can do to help yourself get better, or is there anything you can do to recover? You could even ask if there is something you need to learn or understand.[20]

learn more: http://amzn.to/1rEuRmH

"This exercise is about listening to your intuition, it is said that deep down we know the answers but, because of a busy life, we don't ask and get the answers into our consciousness."

Technique twenty

Gardening

Imagine before you is a garden with big weeds that represent your illness. In your mind, weed the garden until you can see the glorious flowers that represent your health.[21]

learn more: http://amzn.to/13WBWnR

twenty one

Canoeing

For blocked arteries around the heart, a great proven option is this visualisation: close your eyes, take a few deep breaths and imagine yourself shrinking down and entering your body. Once at your heart, visualise yourself canoeing through those arteries and, as you do, begin scraping and removing the blockages. It is recommended that this is done a couple of times a day.[22]

twenty two

Grounding Yourself

Start by counting your breaths from 10 to 0 and, when you feel relaxed, imagine a piece of cord, known as the grounding cord, coming down from the sky, in through your crown, down your spine, into the floor and deep down into the earth below you. Feeling connected to the earth, imagine energy - like that used to help plants grow and prosper - flow up into your body and out through your head.[23]

learn more: http://amzn.to/1rEuRmH

"This grounding exercise is great to help you accept yourself and your situation as it is enabling you to move forward from this point towards your health goal."

Technique twenty three

Illness vs Immune System

Closing your eyes take a few deep breaths and picture your illness - perhaps see it as an animal, food, another person, alien or anything your imagination creates. Then, visualise your immune system, again anything your intuition and mind creates. From here, either during the meditation or after, work out how you can help your immune system do its job of removing illness from the body. Visualise this happening in as many visualisations as you feel you need.[24]
learn more: http://amzn.to/1L7Bt3D

twenty four

Give Thanks

Speak as if you already have what you want as it is much more likely to manifest. For example, "I give thanks for my ever-increasing health, beauty and vitality."[25]

learn more: http://amzn.to/1rEuRmH

Technique twenty five

Personify Your Illness

Picture your illness or condition as a person or creature. For example, if you have a headache you might imagine it as a gremlin that is tightening a vice across your head. Now you have personified your condition, you ask the person or creature a question to find a solution. You can ask the gremlin why it's there and what you can do to make it loosen the vice. Listen to the gremlin's answers. Take its advice and see how things improve.[26]

learn more: http://amzn.to/1BodqGR

twenty six

Treasure Map

Either in your mind, or by drawing, painting or collage, create a map or journey to your ideal situation. Set the route and tasks of things you feel you need to do along the way to get the treasure of your ideal situation. You can then imagine the route and the outcome as many times as you wish.[27]
learn more: http://amzn.to/1rEuRmH

twenty seven

The Boiler

Migraines are where more blood enters the veins in the brain than is let out, causing a build-up of pressure a lot like a faulty boiler. So, let's relax with a few deep breaths and close our eyes to visualise a boiler as a representation of our brain. Perhaps a cartoon boiler which is puffed out in the middle and under pressure. Spotting a dial that can regulate the in and out flow of pressure, turn this dial to the best setting for the boiler and you, setting the boiler back to it most productive and healthy state.[28]
learn more: http://amzn.to/1x8iy2W

twenty eight

True Purpose

Relax with a few deep breaths and imagine yourself on your deathbed, looking back at your life and how you think your life went. "What do you feel your purpose was, or could have been? Or ask yourself the following questions: "If I could do anything in the world, what would I do?", "If I were a millionaire, I would...", "What I love most in the world is...", One thing I would like to change is...".[29]
learn more: http://amzn.to/1rEuRmH

"Knowing our purpose can help us change the way we see the world and behave."

Technique twenty nine

Mental Rehearsal

Just like any Olympic athlete who visualises their goal and has run their race many, many times in their mind before they actually achieve it, you can do the same by relaxing yourself and connecting to your intuition to imagine how your path to recovery will develop. Picture the steps you will take, what each little achievement will be along the way, and how you will feel once you have recovered. Do this as often as you can to instruct your body of your intention.[30]

learn more: http://amzn.to/1D5swC8

Technique thirty

Tension - Twisted Rope

Imagine a thick rope tied between two trees. In the middle of the rope is an iron bar that has been wrapped around and around, making it tighter and tighter - just like an elastic band wound up for a propeller on a toy plane - so tight that the trees are being pulled together. Now, at your own pace, release the tension in the rope by untwisting it with the iron bar. As you do, note how the trees, which represent your body, are released from the tension and are at ease to flow with the wind.[31]

learn more: http://amzn.to/1x8iy2W

"Tension restricts the flow of life - releasing the tension can be very helpful."

thirty one

Life as an Artwork

Picture your life as a piece artwork. Visualise the picture and notice you have the tools to change this picture. You can remove bits, accentuate other parts, and make it exactly as you would like it to be. When you have finished, hang it in the art gallery of your mind to know that is who you can become.[32]
learn more: http://amzn.to/1rEuRmH

"As the Buddha once said, 'We are what we think. All that we are arises with our thoughts. With our thoughts, we make the world.'."

Technique thirty two

Inner Advisor

Inside all of us is a wise yogi who, deep down, knows what is best for us to achieve. Closing your eyes, imagine yourself shrinking down and going inside your body to meet this wise yogi. Go to the place in your body where you would most expect to find the yogi, because that is where he or she will be. Once there, ask any questions you would like to know the answers to. Perhaps you could ask: "What is the best way for me to recover?", "Is there anything you would like me to do?". Just let your questions flow to, and let answers flow from, the yogi. Remember the answers and, after opening your eyes, assess them to see how they can help.[33]

learn more: http://amzn.to/1xByolp

Technique thirty three

The Lake of Health

Closing your eyes, take 3 deep breaths. See yourself looking down on a lake from high on a hill. Send an instruction to the lake that you would like it to reflect your health for your inner and outer body. Stare into the fresh clear water and see yourself inside and out. Note the colours and areas of the body. If you see bright and healthy colours all is good, if you spot areas that are grey or black these are areas you may wish to give some healing attention.[34]
learn more: http://amzn.to/1BkjyAd

"This exercise encourages you to get in touch with, and listen to, your inner intuition."

thirty four

Bubble Technique

Relax yourself with a few deep breaths. Imagine something you would really like to manifest for you. Now, as you see a big colourful bubble floating around you, allow it to surround you with hope. As it does, allow the bubble to begin to float up and out into the universe. Emotionally let go of your vision and allow the universe to take care of manifesting your wish.[35]

learn more: http://amzn.to/1rEuRmH

"As Louise L Hay says, "Trust in the process of life to bring you your highest good."."

thirty five

Burying the Past

Visualise yourself walking a country path that is cluttered and blocked with rubble. Move the rubble out of your way for you to pass. As you walk you find a tree. Sitting down at the tree you see lots of leaves. Pick up the one you are drawn too. On this leaf write everything that has pained you, everything you have thought is holding you back from achieving your goal. Now dig a hole in which to bury this leaf and the past with it. Before burying it, write the date which you would like the leaf to decompose. Walk back down the path, replacing the rubble should you wish too. And note how you feel before opening your eyes.[36]

learn more: http:/linkgoeshere

Golden Healing Light

Sitting or lying down, relax yourself with some deep breaths. Visualise a golden healing light entering your body. Move this light around your body to the places which you feel need it. When in place, imagine the light's heat, size and brightness emitting healing energy. Feel the light, sense it, and imagine each area improving when the light is there.[37]

learn more: http://amzn.to/1rEuRmH

Technique thirty seven

Liberation from Slavery

Enter the world of imagination with reverse breaths - breathing in through the mouth and out through the nose. Notice and feel yourself chained to your illness, see the chains and how they, the kidnappers of your health are hurting you. For example, for asthma, see how this person is pressing their foot on your chest, restricting your breathing. Find the key to the chains to escape this illness or condition. As you undo them and escape, notice how you move from this slavery of illness to the freedom of wellness. [38]

learn more: http://amzn.to/1BodqGR

technique thirty eight

Timeline Healing

Start by relaxing and taking a few deep breaths. Imagine a timeline to your left that goes to the past and to your right that goes to the future. Looking to the left, imagine yourself before your condition - see, feel and experience how you felt. Remember this. Now look to the future, to a time when you have recovered. Once again see, feel and experience that sensation and notice how you feel at achieving this. Now, with your mind, bring the person from the past and merge the old you in this body now, then do the same with the future you. Make sure that the part you wish to recover is aware of how it was and how you want it be.[39]

learn more: http://amzn.to/1ts6wMk

Technique thirty nine

Swap Chairs

Setting 2 chairs opposite each other about 2 metres away, sit on one of the chairs. Imagine a future you, completely recovered, sitting in the other. Examine every part of the future you: your facial expressions, the way you are sitting, and how you think you feel. After a little while, with this image fresh in your mind, go and sit in the other chair. As you sit down imagine your two bodies merging together. Explore how you feel and ensure that the part of your body you want to recover knows exactly what it needs to do for it recover.[40]

learn more: http://amzn.to/1zUdnFQ

Cell Healing

This visualisation focuses on an individual cell. Imagine a cell in your body that needs to repair. Picture it receiving all the nutrients it needs and become aware of it moving in a healthy way. Notice how this one cell has improved and changed. Once you are happy with this cell, ask it to pass the information to the unhealthy cell next to it, notice how this cell becomes healthy, too. Replicate this until you are happy with the results.[41]
learn more: http://amzn.to/1vJg86q

"William Walker Atkinson, in his book 'Mind and Body', said "The cell is a living entity, and does everything that the body does. It eats, drinks, moves and reproduces."."

forty one

Spiritual Affirmations

A magazine called 'Universal Truth' suggests these daily affirmations.

Monday - Perfect health is my external birthright.

Tuesday - I have health of intellect, therefore I have wise judgment and clear understanding.

Wednesday - I am morally healthful, therefore in all my dealings I love to realize that I am quickened by the spirit of integrity.

Thursday - Healthfulness of soul gives me a pure heart and righteousness of motive in everything I do.

Friday - Meditation upon the health of my real being outpictures in physical health and strength, in even temper, joyous spirits and in kind words. [42]
learn more: http://amzn.to/1vJg86q

forty two

Talk and Obey

William Walker Atkinson stated there "is mind in every cell, nerve, organ and part of the body, and in the body as a whole; and this mind will listen to your central mind and obey it.". From one mind to another, send direct instructions of your wish to the part of the body you need to recover. Really feel your intent, desire and feeling being received by this part of the body. Repeat it until you feel the message has been fully absorbed and is being acted upon.[43]
learn more: http://amzn.to/1zUdnFQ

forty three

Affirmation of Health

FW Southworth M.D., in his book "True Metaphysical Science" suggested repeating this affirmation 6 times each day: "As thoughts are not only things, but forces, and act upon our mental and physical life for good or ill, we must be careful to always keep ourselves in that condition of thought which builds up and strengthens, to constantly think thoughts of health, of happiness, of good, to be cheerful, hopeful, confident and fearless.". [44]
learn more: http://amzn.to/1vJg86q

Technique forty four

Autosuggestion

State what you need for recovery and repeat to yourself as many times as you can throughout the day. For example, if you have poor digestion you could say, "I am improving, my stomach is doing its work well, digesting what it is given, the nourishment is assimilated, and it is getting better and better each day.".[45]

learn more: http://amzn.to/1vJg86q

forty five

Munching Rabbit

This could be any animal, however it is a rabbit that worked for Petula. She pictured the rabbit eating and munching away at her cancer cells until she was better. After each session of munching, Petula imagined her rabbit leaving her body to excrete its waste on the same spot nourishing a lovely tree to grow.[46]

learn more: http://amzn.to/1Ael5rP

"Find the best creature for you. It was important for Petula, even in her imagination, not to harm anyone or anything, and this was win-win for her, the rabbit and anyone who was looking for shade."

forty six

Weak to **STRONG!**

As many times as possible throughout the day, think of the part of your body that needs to recover as getting stronger and stronger. If you catch a thought of it as weak, imagine it moving from weak to strong, STRONG, **STRONG!** [47]
learn more: http://amzn.to/1AemhLP

"Doing this empowers you and your body with a belief and intent of recovery."

Technique forty seven

How You Wish to Be

Picture the part of your body you would like to recover, not as it is or how it was, but as it is now and how you wish it to become. In your mind, see, feel and experience it as recovered.[48]

learn more: http://amzn.to/1AemhLP

forty eight

Only Talk of Your Good

It is easy to focus on a pain and illness because it can be a big part of a person's life. The challenge here is to talk to others, and your internal being, about the good things in your life, for example, the gratitude for the healthy parts of your body, your friends, the activities you like doing now, the things you will do once fully recovered, etc.. This sends a message to you, your body and everyone else that you are much more a person than your ailment.[49]
learn more: http://amzn.to/1AemhLP

"If you feel this technique would be helpful, just try it for an hour and notice how you feel, before extending it to hours, days, week or forever."

Technique forty nine

Human Water Filter

Send healing messages and instructions to a glass of water. Instruct the water with what you would like it to do for you. Do this for a couple of minutes, then as you drink it, imagine it going around your body and to the part which needs to recover. Picture the water doing its purpose of sending your message of intent.[50]

learn more: http://amzn.to/1AemhLP

"We are made up of 85% water. Our intention is very important in fulfilling any goal. Intent sets us on the path to our purpose."

Technique fifty

Sources

learn more

All of the following sources are also listed at:
www.possiblemind.co.uk/sources/

Sources - Chapter One

1. You Are the Placebo: Making Your Mind Matter by Dr Joe Dispenza - pg 23 - http://amzn.to/10yu2j3
2. http://www.uncommon-knowledge.co.uk/articles/uncommon-hypnosis/pain-control.html
3. http://www.uncommon-knowledge.co.uk/articles/uncommon-hypnosis/pain-control.html
4. NLP and Relief of Chronic Pain by Libuška Prochazka and Dr Richard Bolstad - http://bit.ly/1e89oxd
5. NLP and Relief of Chronic Pain by Libuška Prochazka and Dr Richard Bolstad - http://bit.ly/1e89oxd
6. Chronic pain is like...The clinical use of analogy... - Rachael Coakley and Neil Schechter - http://bit.ly/1TgelUI
7. Health Magazine (Autumn 2011)- Using NLP to... help with Pain - http://bit.ly/1f6D2TT
8. Theory and Practice of Brief Therapy - By Simon H. Budman, Alan S. Gurman - pg 212 - http://amzn.to/1pRDPpi
9. Theory and Practice of Brief Therapy - By Simon H. Budman, Alan S. Gurman - pg 212 - http://amzn.to/1pRDPpi
10. http://www.uncommon-knowledge.co.uk/articles/uncommon-hypnosis/pain-control.html
11. How your mind can heal your body - David R. Hamilton - pg 20 - http://amzn.to/1rV5Ama
12. How your mind can heal your body - David R. Hamilton - pg 20 - http://amzn.to/1rV5Ama
13. How your mind can heal your body - David R. Hamilton - pg 22 - http://amzn.to/1rV5Ama
14. How your mind can heal your body - David R. Hamilton - pg 26 - http://amzn.to/1rV5Ama
15. How your mind can heal your body - David R. Hamilton - pg 26 - http://amzn.to/1rV5Ama
16. The Trojan Horse of Pain - Pain: A Political History by Keith Wailoo - Section 1 - http://amzn.to/Z1gs6j
17. Your mind can heal your body - Matthew Manning - pg 81 - http://amzn.to/1rVMzkR
18. Your mind can heal your body - Matthew Manning - pg 81 - http://amzn.to/1rVMzkR
19. Your mind can heal your body - Matthew Manning - pg 81 - http://amzn.to/1rVMzkR
20. Wonderpedia Magazine - April 2014 - pg 14 - http://bit.ly/1MOh0At
21. Wonderpedia Magazine - April 2014 - pg 14 - http://bit.ly/1MOh0At
22. Dissolving Pain: Simple Brain-Training Exercises for Chronic Pain - Les Femi - pg 23 - http://amzn.to/1CKbfiC
23. The Brain That Changes Itself: Stories of Personal Triump... - Norman Doidge - Chapter 3 - http://amzn.to/1tSMVdB
24. Dissolving Pain: Simple Brain-Training Exercises for Chronic Pain - Les Femi - pg 28 - http://amzn.to/1CKbfiC
25. Dissolving Pain: Simple Brain-Training Exercises for Chronic Pain - Les Femi - pg 52 - http://amzn.to/1CKbfiC
26. Dissolving Pain: Simple Brain-Training Exercises for Chronic Pain - Les Femi - pg 69 - http://amzn.to/1CKbfiC
27. Hypnotize Yourself Out of Pain Now! - Bruce N. Eimer - pg36 - http://amzn.to/1rV63Vw
28. Dissolving Pain: Simple Brain-Training Exercises for Chronic Pain - Les Femi - pg 76 - http://amzn.to/1CKbfiC
29. Dissolving Pain: Simple Brain-Training Exercises for Chronic Pain - Les Femi - pg 137 - http://amzn.to/1CKbfiC
30. Dissolving Pain: Simple Brain-Training Exercises for Chronic Pain - Les Femi - pg 137 - http://amzn.to/1CKbfiC
31. Hypnotize Yourself Out of Pain Now! - Bruce N. Eimer - pg - Preface xxxv - http://amzn.to/1rV63Vw
32. Hypnotize Yourself Out of Pain Now! - Bruce N. Eimer - pg18 - http://amzn.to/1rV63Vw
33. Hypnotize Yourself Out of Pain Now! - Bruce N. Eimer - pg35 - http://amzn.to/1rV63Vw
34. Hypnotize Yourself Out of Pain Now! - Bruce N. Eimer - pg186 - http://amzn.to/1rV63Vw
35. Break Through Pain - Shinzen Young - pg 2 - http://amzn.to/1rVN8Lz
36. Possible Mind Website - Pain Relief with Virtual Reality - http://bit.ly/1FeoFSl
37. http://www.transformations.net.nz/trancescript/nlp-and-relief-of-chronic-pain.html
38. Possible Mind Website - Noesitherapy Pain Control by Dr Escudero - http://bit.ly/1uZ73Fp
39. Hypnosis and Suggestion in the Treatment of Pain by Barber, Hilgard - pg 73 - http://amzn.to/1s0ystC
40. Scientific American Mind - September/October 2013 - pg 20 - http://bit.ly/1L4WHRj
41. Scientific American Mind - September/October 2013 - pg 20 - http://bit.ly/1L4WHRj
42. http://www.reading.ac.uk/news-and-events/releases/PR590186.aspx
43. Hypnosis and Suggestion in the Treatment of Pain by Barber, Hilgard - pg 8 - http://amzn.to/1s0ystC
44. The Placebo Effect in Clinical Practice by Walter A. Brown - pg 31 - http://amzn.to/1vHap2R
45. The Placebo Effect in Clinical Practice by Walter A. Brown - pg 32 - http://amzn.to/1vHap2R
46. http://painconsortium.nih.gov/symptomresearch/chapter_1/sec2/cmms2pg1.htm
47. http://www.sciencedaily.com/releases/2011/02/110226212356.htm
48. http://www.columbia.edu/cu/news/04/03/placebo_effect.html
49. Unlearn Your Pain by Howard Schubiner MD - http://amzn.to/1tmKeju
50. http://www.stitchlinks.com/research1.html

Sources - Chapter Two

1. Relaxation Techniques: Teach Yourself by Alice Muir - http://amzn.to/ZKLS1q
2. Hypnotize Yourself Out of Pain Now! - Bruce N. Eimer pg 141 - http://amzn.to/1whmOtB
3. http://articles.mercola.com/sites/articles/archive/2013/07/04/13-mind-body-techniques.aspx
4. Trauma Competency: A Clinician's Guide by Linda Curren - pg 162 - http://amzn.to/1zgM0G6
5. Hypnotize Yourself Out of Pain Now! - Bruce N. Eimer pg 141 - http://amzn.to/1whmOtB
6. Emotional First Aid: Healing Rejection, Guilt, Failure, and Other Everyday... by Guy Winch - http://amzn.to/1uoxHYf
7. http://www.wikihow.com/Overcome-Physical-Pain-With-Your-Mind
8. Time Line Therapy and the Basis of Personality by Tad James - http://amzn.to/ZAQzL0
9. http://www.babycenter.com/0_moms-say-top-pain-management-techniques-during-labor_10339940.bc
10. http://www.babycenter.com/0_moms-say-top-pain-management-techniques-during-labor_10339940.bc
11. Hypnotize Yourself Out of Pain Now! - Bruce N. Eimer pg 141 - http://amzn.to/1whmOtB
12. Noesitherapy Mind Over Matter Pain Control & Psychological Healing... by Brian Howard - http://amzn.to/1tCUvsI
13. http://www.spine-health.com/conditions/chronic-pain/11-chronic-pain-control-techniques
14. Hypnotize Yourself Out of Pain Now! - Bruce N. Eimer pg 141 - http://amzn.to/1whmOtB
15. http://www.spine-health.com/conditions/chronic-pain/11-chronic-pain-control-techniques
16. http://www.spine-health.com/conditions/chronic-pain/11-chronic-pain-control-techniques
17. http://www.spine-health.com/conditions/chronic-pain/11-chronic-pain-control-techniques
18. http://www.spine-health.com/conditions/chronic-pain/11-chronic-pain-control-techniques
19. http://www.spine-health.com/conditions/chronic-pain/11-chronic-pain-control-techniques
20. http://www.spine-health.com/conditions/chronic-pain/11-chronic-pain-control-techniques
21. http://www.spine-health.com/conditions/chronic-pain/11-chronic-pain-control-techniques
22. Hypnotize Yourself Out of Pain Now! - Bruce N. Eimer pg 141 - http://amzn.to/1whmOtB
23. http://www.spine-health.com/conditions/chronic-pain/11-chronic-pain-control-techniques
24. How to Wake Up: A Buddhist-Inspired Guide to Navigating Jo... by Toni Bernhard pg 89 - http://amzn.to/1yOPTB0
25. How to Wake Up: A Buddhist-Inspired Guide to Navigating Jo... by Toni Bernhard pg 89 - http://amzn.to/1yOPTB0
26. Full Catastrophe Living by Jon Kabat-Zinn - http://amzn.to/1zgMgow
27. Imagine Yourself Well - by Sean F. Kelly - http://amzn.to/1wdmQDN
28. Imagine Yourself Well - by Sean F. Kelly - http://amzn.to/1wdmQDN
29. http://www.uncommon-knowledge.co.uk/articles/uncommon-hypnosis/pain-control.html
30. http://www.cncahealth.com/explore/learn/mind-body-health/nine-strategies-for-easing-pain-without-drugs
31. http://www.cncahealth.com/explore/learn/mind-body-health/nine-strategies-for-easing-pain-without-drugs
32. Advanced Mental Techniques for Pain Relief: Self-Ther... by Shlomo Vaknin C.Ht pg 105 - http://amzn.to/1tCUVzh
33. Hypnotize Yourself Out of Pain Now! - Bruce N. Eimer - Pg 111 - http://amzn.to/1whmOtB
34. Dissolving Pain - A new approach to pain - Les Femi Ph.d pg 109 - http://amzn.to/1qTL2X7
35. Handbook of Hypnotic Suggestions and Metaphors by Harold B. Crasilneck pg 485 - http://amzn.to/1uozrkc
36. Hypnotize Yourself Out of Pain Now! - Bruce N. Eimer - Pg 117 - http://amzn.to/1whmOtB
37. http://www.transformations.net.nz/trancescript/nlp-and-relief-of-chronic-pain.html
38. Hypnotize Yourself Out of Pain Now! - Bruce N. Eimer - Pg 133 - http://amzn.to/1whmOtB
39. http://www.hypnosis101.com/hypnosis-tips/time-distortion/
40. Hypnotize Yourself Out of Pain Now! - Bruce N. Eimer - Pg 133 - http://amzn.to/1whmOtB
41. Hypnosis In The Relief Of Pain by Ernest R. Hilgard, Josephine R. Hilgard - http://amzn.to/1ylmIrL
42. Hypnotize Yourself Out of Pain Now! - Bruce N. Eimer - Pg 134 - http://amzn.to/1whmOtB
43. Hypnotize Yourself Out of Pain Now! - Bruce N. Eimer - Pg 119 - http://amzn.to/1whmOtB
44. Hypnotize Yourself Out of Pain Now! - Bruce N. Eimer - Pg 84 - http://amzn.to/1whmOtB
45. Hypnotize Yourself Out of Pain Now! - Bruce N. Eimer - Pg 98 - http://amzn.to/1whmOtB
46. Hypnotize Yourself Out of Pain Now! - Bruce N. Eimer - Pg 114 - http://amzn.to/1whmOtB
47. Hypnotize Yourself Out of Pain Now! - Bruce N. Eimer - Pg 137 - http://amzn.to/1whmOtB
48. Hypnotize Yourself Out of Pain Now! - Bruce N. Eimer - Pg 132 - http://amzn.to/1whmOtB
49. Hypnotize Yourself Out of Pain Now! - Bruce N. Eimer - Pg 125 - http://amzn.to/1whmOtB
50. Hypnotize Yourself Out of Pain Now! - Bruce N. Eimer - Pg 112 - http://amzn.to/1whmOtB

Sources - Chapter Three

1. http://www.nejm.org/doi/full/10.1056/NEJMoa013259
2. Remarkable Recovery: What Extraordinary Healings Tell Us...- by Marc Ian Barasch - http://amzn.to/1s9r0x7
3. http://www.healingcancernaturally.com/power-of-thought-to-heal-1.html
4. http://blog.placeboeffect.com/placebo-experiment/ and http://www.ncbi.nlm.nih.gov/pubmed/10190407
5. http://www.healingcancernaturally.com/power-of-thought-to-heal-1.html
6. How your mind can heal your body - David R. Hamilton - pg 24 - http://amzn.to/10Giv10
7. Results international Audio - 9:55 secs - http://possiblemind.co.uk/mind-changers-for-the-body-and-health/
8. Results international Audio - 9:26secs - http://possiblemind.co.uk/mind-changers-for-the-body-and-health/
9. www.dailymail.co.uk/health/article-2003267/Cancer-Hypnotism-speeds-op-recovery-cuts-chance-returning.html
10. How your mind can heal your body - David R. Hamilton - pg 5 - http://amzn.to/10Giv10
11. How your mind can heal your body - David R. Hamilton - pg 23 - http://amzn.to/10Giv10
12. How your mind can heal your body - David R. Hamilton - pg 26 - http://amzn.to/10Giv10
13. How your mind can heal your body - David R. Hamilton - pg 27 - http://amzn.to/10Giv10
14. How your mind can heal your body - David R. Hamilton - pg 66 - http://amzn.to/10Giv10
15. How your mind can heal your body - David R. Hamilton - pg 67 - http://amzn.to/10Giv10
16. How your mind can heal your body - David R. Hamilton - pg 75 - http://amzn.to/10Giv10
17. How your mind can heal your body - David R. Hamilton - pg 77 - http://amzn.to/10Giv10
18. How your mind can heal your body - David R. Hamilton - pg 77 - http://amzn.to/10Giv10
19. How your mind can heal your body - David R. Hamilton - pg 81 - http://amzn.to/10Giv10
20. How your mind can heal your body - David R. Hamilton - pg 83 - http://amzn.to/10Giv10
21. Your mind can heal your body - Matthew Manning - pg5 - http://amzn.to/10Gjkai
22. Your mind can heal your body - Matthew Manning - pg11 - http://amzn.to/10Gjkai
23. Your mind can heal your body - Matthew Manning - pg11 - http://amzn.to/10Gjkai
24. Your mind can heal your body - Matthew Manning - pg16 - http://amzn.to/10Gjkai
25. Your mind can heal your body - Matthew Manning - pg25 - http://amzn.to/10Gjkai
26. Your mind can heal your body - Matthew Manning - pg37 - http://amzn.to/10Gjkai
27. Your mind can heal your body - Matthew Manning - pg55 - http://amzn.to/10Gjkai
28. Your mind can heal your body - Matthew Manning - pg55 - http://amzn.to/10Gjkai
29. Your mind can heal your body - Matthew Manning - pg55- http://amzn.to/10Gjkai
30. Your mind can heal your body - Matthew Manning - pg61 - http://amzn.to/10Gjkai
31. Your mind can heal your body - Matthew Manning - pg87 - http://amzn.to/10Gjkai
32. Your mind can heal your body - Matthew Manning - pg99 - http://amzn.to/10Gjkai
33. Your mind can heal your body - Matthew Manning - pg124- http://amzn.to/10Gjkai
34. Your mind can heal your body - Matthew Manning - pg138 - http://amzn.to/10Gjkai
35. Your mind can heal your body - Matthew Manning - pg159 - http://amzn.to/10Gjkai
36. Why Me? Harnessing the Healing Power of the Human... - G Porter & P. A. Norris -pg 2 - http://amzn.to/1vIIL45
37. Why Me? Harnessing the Healing Power of the Human...- G Porter & P. A. Norris -pg 127 - http://amzn.to/1vIIL45
38. Why Me? Harnessing the Healing Power of the Human...- G Porter & P. A. Norris -pg 128 - http://amzn.to/1vIIL45
39. Why Me? Harnessing the Healing Power of the Human...- G Porter & P. A. Norris -pg 128 - http://amzn.to/1vIIL45
40. Why Me? Harnessing the Healing Power of the Human...- G Porter & P. A. Norris -pg 160 - http://amzn.to/1vIIL45
41. http://www.ncbi.nlm.nih.gov/pmc/articles/PMC2515569/
42. http://www.nytimes.com/1985/05/21/science/new-focus-on-multiple-personality.html
43. #9 http://listverse.com/2013/05/21/10-amazing-examples-of-mind-over-matter/
44. Theory and Practice of Brief Therapy By Simon H. Budman, Alan S. Gurman - pg194 http://amzn.to/1rdO4Vc
45. #8 http://listverse.com/2013/05/21/10-amazing-examples-of-mind-over-matter/
46. #7 http://listverse.com/2013/05/21/10-amazing-examples-of-mind-over-matter/
47. #2 http://listverse.com/2013/05/21/10-amazing-examples-of-mind-over-matter/
48. #4 http://listverse.com/2013/05/21/10-amazing-examples-of-mind-over-matter/
49. http://www.dailymail.co.uk/femail/article-2240482/Overweight-woman-uses-gastric-band-hypnosis-lose-55lbs-diagnosed-polio-like-syndrome.html
50. It's All in Your Mind by Noel Cox - http://amzn.to/1pIgzuH

Sources - Chapter Four

1. Mind Over Medicine: Scientific Proof That You Can Heal Yourself - Lissa Rankin M.D. - http://amzn.to/13KZM5q
2. pg 12 - Healing Visualizations: Creating Health Through Imagery – Gerald Epstein - http://amzn.to/13WBWnR
3. pg - 119 - How your mind can heal your body - David R. Hamilton - http://amzn.to/1Ael5rP
4. pg 108 - Mind and Body: Mental States and Physical Conditi... - William Walker Atkinson - http://amzn.to/1vJg86q
5. pg - 122 - How your mind can heal your body - David R. Hamilton - http://amzn.to/1Ael5rP
6. pg 45 - The Magic Power of Mental Images – Dean Amory - http://amzn.to/1BodqGR
7. pg - 123 - How your mind can heal your body - David R. Hamilton - http://amzn.to/1Ael5rP
8. pg 14 - Healing Visualizations: Creating Health Through Imagery – Gerald Epstein - http://amzn.to/13WBWnR
9. pg - 122 - How your mind can heal your body - David R. Hamilton - http://amzn.to/1Ael5rP
10. .1) Voluntary Controls – Jack Schwarz - http://amzn.to/1ts5Arm
    .2) Creative Visualization - Shakti Gawain - pg 145 - http://amzn.to/1rEuRmH
11. pg - 132 - How your mind can heal your body - David R. Hamilton - http://amzn.to/1Ael5rP
12. http://www.hypnosis-kids.com/hypnosis-magic-eraser.htm
13. pg - 147 - How your mind can heal your body - David R. Hamilton - http://amzn.to/1Ael5rP
14. pg 156 - Heal Yourself!: How to Harness Placebo Powe - Beverly Potter & Mark Estren - http://amzn.to/1L7Bt3D
15. pg - 164 / 168 - How your mind can heal your body - David R. Hamilton - http://amzn.to/1Ael5rP
16. Living Well With Pain And Illness - Vidyamala Burch - http://amzn.to/1GRtsQK
17. Mind Over Medicine: Scientific Proof That You Can Heal Yourself - Lissa Rankin M.D. - http://amzn.to/13KZM5q
18. pg - 223 - How your mind can heal your body - David R. Hamilton - http://amzn.to/1Ael5rP
19. pg 117 - Heal Yourself!: How to Harness Placebo Powe - Beverly Potter & Mark Estren - http://amzn.to/1L7Bt3D
20. pg 100 - Creative Visualization - Shakti Gawain - http://amzn.to/1rEuRmH
21. pg 8 - Healing Visualizations: Creating Health Through Imagery – Gerald Epstein - http://amzn.to/13WBWnR
22. Results international training session - http://possiblemind.co.uk/mind-changers-for-the-body-and-health/
23. pg 89 - Creative Visualization - Shakti Gawain - http://amzn.to/1rEuRmH
24. pg 117 - Heal Yourself!: How to Harness Placebo Powe - Beverly Potter & Mark Estren - http://amzn.to/1L7Bt3D
25. pg 100 - Creative Visualization - Shakti Gawain - http://amzn.to/1rEuRmH
26. pg 45 - The Magic Power of Mental Images – Dean Amory - http://amzn.to/1BodqGR
27. pg 147 - Creative Visualization - Shakti Gawain - http://amzn.to/1rEuRmH
28. pg 325 - Imagine Yourself Well - Sean F. Kelly - http://amzn.to/1x8iy2W
29. pg 168 - Creative Visualization - Shakti Gawain - http://amzn.to/1rEuRmH
30. You Are the Placebo: Making Your Mind Matter - Dr Joe Dispenza - http://amzn.to/1D5swC8
31. pg 325 - Imagine Yourself Well - Sean F. Kelly - http://amzn.to/1x8iy2W
32. pg 170 - Creative Visualization - Shakti Gawain - http://amzn.to/1rEuRmH
33. pg 92 / 229 - Guided Imagery for Self-healing – by Martin L. Rossman - http://amzn.to/1xByolp
34. pg 107 - Handbook of Therapeutic Imagery Techniques - Anees Ahmad Sheikh - http://amzn.to/1BkjyAd
35. pg 98 - Creative Visualization - Shakti Gawain - http://amzn.to/1rEuRmH
36. pg 108 - Handbook of Therapeutic Imagery Techniques - Anees Ahmad Sheikh - http://amzn.to/1BkjyAd
37. pg 100 - Creative Visualization by Shakti Gawain - http://amzn.to/1rEuRmH
38. pg 46 - The Magic Power of Mental Images – by Dean Amory - http://amzn.to/1BodqGR
39. pg 112 - The New Hypnotherapy Handbook: Hypnosis and Mind Body H... - Kevin Hogan - http://amzn.to/1ts6wMk
40. pg 287 - Mind Power: The Secret of Mental Magic - William Walker Atkinson - http://amzn.to/1zUdnFQ
41. pg 33 - Mind and Body: Mental States and Physical Conditions - William Walker Atkinson - http://amzn.to/1vJg86q
42. pg 94 - Mind and Body: Mental States and Physical Conditions - William Walker Atkinson - http://amzn.to/1vJg86q
43. pg 294 - Mind Power: The Secret of Mental Magic - William Walker Atkinson - http://amzn.to/1zUdnFQ
44. pg 99 - Mind and Body: Mental States and Physical Conditions - William Walker Atkinson - http://amzn.to/1vJg86q
45. pg 101 - Mind and Body: Mental States and Physical Conditions - William Walker Atkinson - http://amzn.to/1vJg86q
46. pg - 121 - How your mind can heal your body - David R. Hamilton - http://amzn.to/1Ael5rP
47. pg 29 - Self-Healing by Thought Force – William Walker Atkinson - http://amzn.to/1AemhLP
48. pg 30 - Self-Healing by Thought Force – William Walker Atkinson - http://amzn.to/1AemhLP
49. pg 35 - Self-Healing by Thought Force – William Walker Atkinson - http://amzn.to/1AemhLP
50. pg 16 - Self-Healing by Thought Force – William Walker Atkinson - http://amzn.to/1AemhLP